CW00520647

JUDI DENCH

A Life in the Spotlight

Daniel K. Mealy

Table of Content

Introduction

Introduction

There are shining stars who leave an indelible impression on the entertainment industry and transcend the boundaries of stage and screen throughout the history of theater and film. Among these legends, Dame Judi Dench stands out as a unique and enduring personality, demonstrating through her life the transformational power of skill, commitment, and sheer willpower. From the enthralling peaks of her stage performances to the nuanced depths of her film depictions, Judi Dench has not only shone a spotlight on herself but has also evolved into a brilliant beacon of the performing arts.

Chapter 1: Early Years

On the stage, where aspirations are realized, a young woman by the name of Judith Olivia Dench began her quest to become a living legend. Judi Dench was born on December 9th, 1934 in York, England. She displayed an early innate affinity for the performing arts that would impact her entire life.

Judi was introduced to theater at a young age since her family loved culture and the arts. Her father, Reginald Arthur Dench, was a physician, and her mother, Eleanora Olive Jones, was a costume mistress at the York Theatre. Young Judi had access to the realm of creativity and imagination thanks to her family's involvement in the theater.

Her early years were characterized by a mix of curiosity and tenacity. She first fell in love with acting while attending the Mount School in York, an independent Quaker school. She actively engaged in school plays as a student, setting the groundwork for what would later develop into a dazzling career.

Early Judi Dench's theater involvement went beyond the stage at her school. She joined neighborhood theater companies, such as the York Mystery Plays, where she developed her skills and started to demonstrate her extraordinary aptitude. Even in those formative years, her natural ability to become a character and enthrall audiences was clear.

However, her route to prominence was not without its hurdles. Dench lost her mother when she was 16 years old, which was a traumatic sorrow that profoundly influenced her outlook on life and acting. But she persisted, propelled by her enthusiasm and inspired by the principles her mother had taught her.

Dench's commitment to her trade as she grew older got her accepted to London's famous Central School of Speech and Drama. She underwent professional instruction and honed her skills under the guidance of renowned acting teachers, which was a pivotal period in her life.

Dench responded to the pull of the London theater scene with unrelenting tenacity. At the Old Vic Theatre, she made her professional debut in 1957, an important milestone that launched her career as a star. Her rise in the theater industry would then be nothing short of stratospheric.

Judi Dench's early acting enthusiasm was intense, and audiences and critics alike started to take notice of her unrelenting dedication to her work. Little did the world realize that this young York girl would grow up to become one of her generation's most renowned and talented actors?

Childhood and Family Background

On December 9, 1934, Judi Dench was born in York, Britain, and went on to become a well-known performing artist whose title has come to speak to brilliance in both theater and movies. She was the most youthful of her family's three children, and her full title at birth was Judith Olivia Dench. Eleanora Olive (née Jones), her mother, was a closet special lady, and her father, Reginald Arthur Dench, was a doctor. The bizarre mixing of dramatic and restorative impacts in Judi Dench's family would along these lines have an enormous effect on her life and work.

Youthful Judi Dench was introduced to performing expressions at an early age, developing up within the small town of Haworth in Yorkshire, Britain. Her father, a doctor in preparation, worked as the theater's inhabitant restorative officer, and both of her guardians were passionate theatergoers. This affiliation with the performing expressions and theater would be pivotal to Judi's future course.

Her mother deplorably passed away when she was 10 a long time ago, having a noteworthy impact on her. Consistent in her life, her father gave her and her kin a kind and empowering domestic life. Due to her father's engagement in territorial beginner theater plays, Judi was propelled to seek after the expressions amid these developments for a long time.

She went to York's Mount School as a young child, where her cherishing of acting proceeded to develop. She created the arrangement as a result of her inclusion in school plays and her early presentation to York's flourishing showy community.

In hindsight, her early life and her family's history made the foundation for her extraordinary career. Judi Dench's change into the famous performing artist she would become was affected by a few components, including her mother's interest in theater, her father's preparation for medication, and the adoring climate her family provided. Because of her early introduction to the theater and common aptitude, she finally joined the Illustrious Shakespeare Company and embarked on a mind-blowing enterprise within the highlight.

Early Education and Theater Beginnings

Dench's instructive way played an essential part in sustaining her budding ability. She attended Mount School in York, an all-girls Quaker school with a wealthy convention of advancing inventiveness and personal expression. It was at Mount School where Dench's adoration for acting was, to begin with, aroused. She took part in school plays and sharpened her acting aptitudes in this supporting environment.

Her early encounters at the school were arranged not as they uncovered her characteristic ability but to foreshadow her future victory. Her instructors recognized her uncommon capacities and energized her to seek a career in acting. Dench's family, eminently her guardians, upheld her desires, understanding the importance of cultivating her enthusiasm.

Upon completing her education at Mount School, Judi Dench took her first steps towards a proficient acting career. She enlisted in London's Central School of Discourse and Show, a famous institution that has delivered numerous famous performing artists. This formal preparation permitted her to refine her craft, create her voice, and pick up a more profound understanding of emotional hypotheses.

It wasn't long ago that Dench's ability caught the attention of theater executives. She made her proficient stage debut in 1957 at the Ancient Vic Theater in London, a prestigious setting known for sustaining developing ability. Her execution as Ophelia in Shakespeare's "Villa" stamped the starting of an exceptional journey within the world of theater.

All through the late 1950s and early 1960s, Dench kept on seeing groups of onlookers and faultfinders with her flexibility on the stage. Her capacity to bring depth and realness to a wide run of characters showcased her monstrous potential as an on-screen character. She got to be a noticeable figure within the British theater scene, gaining basic approval and building a steadfast fan base.

Her commitment to her make and her commitment to sharpening her skills would eventually move her to universal recognition, making her one of the foremost regarded and celebrated performing artists of her era.

Chapter 2: Rising Star

Her reputation as one of the most gifted and promising actors in Britain began to solidify during this time.

Judi Dench joined the famed Royal Shakespeare Company (RSC), which marked the beginning of her ascent to stardom.

Entry into the Royal Shakespeare Company

Judi Dench's passage into the Illustrious Shakespeare Company checked an essential minute in her career and played a critical part in forming her into the famous on-screen character we know nowadays. Born in 1934 in York, Britain, Dench's early presentation to the world of theater and her uncommon ability cleared the way for this surprising journey.

From a youthful age, Dench showed an enthusiasm for acting and a profound appreciation for the works of William Shakespeare. Her guardians, both of whom were included in neighborhood novice theater preparations, empowered her. As a youngster, she went to the Mount School in York, an institution known for its center on show and expression, which supported her burgeoning talent.

In 1957, at the age of 23, Judi Dench tried out for the Illustrious Shakespeare Company (RSC), a prestigious theater organization eminent for its commitment to Shakespearean preparations and classical theater. Her tryout was a resonating victory, and she was advertised a contract with the RSC, stamping the start of her proficient acting career.

Dench's early long time with the RSC was checked by her commitment to the making of acting and her assurance to exceed expectations in classical parts. She made her RSC debut in 1961 as Ophelia in "Villa," a part that showcased her surprising capacity to communicate complex feelings and earned her basic recognition. Her exhibitions in Shakespearean classics like "Macbeth," "Romeo and Juliet," and "Twelfth Night" assisted her notoriety as a talented Shakespearean actress.

One of the characterizing highlights of Dench's time with the RSC was her flexibility as an on-screen character. Whereas she was celebrated for her Shakespearean parts, she moreover grasped modern and cutting-edge theater, illustrating her flexibility and run. This flexibility permitted her to exceed expectations in both classical and modern preparations, making her a standout ability inside the RSC and the broader theater community.

Throughout her residency with the RSC, Judi Dench sharpened her mark, worked with nearby regarded actors and executives, and proceeded to get basic recognition for her exhibitions. Her commitment to the arrangement and her capacity to epitomize characters with profundity and realness set her apart as one of the company's brightest stars.

Judi Dench's section in the Regal Shakespeare Company not only propelled her famous career but also cemented her status as a driving performing artist of her era. Her time with the RSC was stamped by imaginative development and an extending appreciation for the control of theater, setting the organizer for the famous parts and honors that would take a long time to come.

Notable Stage Performances

Dench's capacity to charm groups of onlookers with her commanding nearness, enthusiastic profundity, and immaculate conveyance has cleared out a permanent check on the world of theater.

One of the characterizing minutes in Judi Dench's organized career was her affiliation with the Illustrious Shakespeare Company (RSC). She joined the RSC in the late 1950s and rapidly got to be an unmistakable part of the troupe. Her depiction of notorious Shakespearean characters like Ophelia in "Village" and Woman Macbeth in

"Macbeth" showcased her flexibility and capacity to breathe life into complex roles.

In 1965, Dench took on the part of Titania in Diminish Hall's generation of "A Midsummer Night's Dream." Her charming and ethereal execution earned her far-reaching recognition and set her up as a driving Shakespearean on-screen character. This generation was a turning point in her career and set the stage for her future successes.

Dench's depiction of Cleopatra in "Antony and Cleopatra" encouraged her notoriety as an imposing Shakespearean on-screen character. Her attractive organized nearness and passionate escalation brought profundity to this famous character. Groups of onlookers and pundits alike were enchanted by her execution, making it one of the standout minutes in her dramatic journey.

Beyond Shakespeare, Dench has moreover exceeded expectations in modern and classic theater. Her depiction of Banter Bowles within the melodic "Cabaret" earned her a Laurence Olivier Grant, displaying her flexibility in both emotional and melodic parts. Her translation of the strong-willed Barbara Undershaft in George Bernard Shaw's "Major Barbara" showed her dominance of classic theater, winning her another wave of acclaim.

In the 1980s and 1990s, Dench kept on sparkling on arrange, taking on parts in plays like "Absolute Hell" and "Amy's See." Her capacity to put through with groups of onlookers on an enthusiastic level, in any case of the character or genre, set her apart as a genuine showy luminary.

Notably, her depiction of Ruler Elizabeth I in the play "Shakespeare in Adore" brought her worldwide recognition. Whereas the play investigated the imaginative handle behind Shakespeare's works, Dench's execution as the formidable monarch was a standout minute, winning her a Foundation Grant for Best Supporting Actress.

Her career in the organization could be a confirmation of her exceptional ability and devotion to her creation. Her capacity to epitomize a wide run of characters, from Shakespearean heroines to modern figures, has cleared a permanent stamp on the world of theater. Her bequest as one of the most prominent arranged on-screen characters of all time isn't as it was characterized by her various grants but also by the profound impact she has had on gatherings of people and individual on-screen characters alike, motivating eras to come to grasp the craftsmanship of the stage.

Chapter 3: Transition to Film

Judi Dench's travel from the theater to the silver screen stamped an urgent chapter in her distinguished career. Whereas she had built up herself as an eminent organized performing artist, her move to film opened up modern roads for her creative expression and brought her gifts to a worldwide gathering of people.

Film Debut and Early Movie Roles

Judi Dench's raid into the world of cinema stamped an essential minute in her distinguished career, opening up modern skylines and uncovering her exceptional gifts to a more extensive group of onlookers. Her film made a big appearance and early motion picture parts showcased her flexibility as a performing artist and set the stage for a fruitful move from the theater to the silver screen.

Dench's to begin with steps into the world of film came within the 1960s, a period characterized by the British Unused Wave in cinema. Her big appearance in the film was "The Third Mystery" in 1964, where she played a supporting part. Even though her starting wander into film was generally unassuming, it laid the establishment for what would end up a momentous cinematic journey.

In the long time that took after, Judi Dench took on an extent of different parts in different classes, setting her notoriety as an on-screen character of uncommon profundity and expertise. Her early motion picture parts showcased her capacity to adjust to diverse characters and classes, from show to comedy and everything in between.

One of her breakthrough minutes in cinema was her part in "A Room with a See" (1985), an adjustment of E.M. Forster's novel. Dench's depiction of the unconventional writer Eleanor Extravagant earned her basic approval and built her up as a constraint to be figured within the film industry. This stamped the starting of an arrangement of unmistakable parts in scholarly adjustments, a sort where she would exceed expectations all through her career.

Another significant early part was in "Mrs. Brown" (1997), in which she played Ruler Victoria inverse, Billy Connolly. Her execution in this film earned broad acknowledgment, winning her the BAFTA Award for Best On-screen Character in a

Driving Part and her to begin with Foundation Grant designation. It was a confirmation of her capacity to occupy complex authentic characters and breathe life into them.

During this stage of her career, Dench showed up in movies like "Shakespeare in Adore" (1998), for which she won a Foundation Grant for Best Supporting On-screen Character, and "Chocolate" (2000). These advancements set her status as a regarded figure within the film industry and made her an adored on-screen character on both sides of the Atlantic.

Judi Dench's film made a big appearance and early motion picture parts were a confirmation of her flexibility and creative run. These developmental encounters in cinema cleared the way for her to end up one of the foremost celebrated and persevering on-screen characters within the history of film, setting the arrange for a career filled with notorious exhibitions and various awards. Her capacity to consistently move from the organization to the screen was a confirmation of her uncommon ability and stamped the starting of a cinematic bequest that proceeds to charm gatherings of people to this day.

Recognition in Hollywood

While Judi had as of presently built up herself as a respected on-screen character inside the British theater and film industry, her move to Hollywood brought her capacity to the around-the-world group of onlookers. Dench's Hollywood travels began with her part as Ruler Victoria in the 1997 film "Mrs.

Brown. This delineation earned her around-the-world acknowledgment and checked her as a compel to be figured with inside the film industry. Her execution was not because it was in a general sense acclaimed but moreover earned several prestigious awards and assignments, including a Foundation Grant assignment for Best On-screen character.

Following her triumph in "Mrs. Brown," Dench kept on surprising Hollywood bunches of spectators with her earth-shattering acting capacities. One of her most celebrated parts came when she delineated M, the head of MI6, inside the James Bond film course of action, starting with "GoldenEye" in 1995. Her portrayal of M included significance and gravitas to the character, making her an in a general sense parcel of the Bond foundation for over two decades. Her closeness in these motion pictures contrasted with the Bond course of action and showcased her adaptability as an actress.

Dench's capacity to reliably move between diverse sorts and character sorts helped cement her status in Hollywood. She took on challenging and differentiating parts in movement pictures like "Chocolat" (2000), "Iris" (2001), and "Notes on a Disgrace" (2006). Her introductions dependably earned basic acknowledgment and braced her position as one of the industry's most regarded actresses.

In confirmation of her unprecedented commitments to Hollywood, Dench received diverse gifts, checking different Foundation Allow assignments and a win for Best

Supporting On-screen Character in "Shakespeare in Respect" (1998). She has also received several Brilliant Globe Grants and BAFTA Grants for her shocking work in both driving and supporting roles.

Beyond her gifts and assignments, Judi Dench's closeness in Hollywood brought a level of radiance and legitimacy to any amplify she was a portion of. Her title needed to be synonymous with enormity in acting, and makers looked to collaborate with her, knowing that her consideration would overhaul the quality of their preparations.

Judi Dench's affirmation in Hollywood was not near to her capacity but additionally her enduring task and capacity to charm bunches of spectators all over the globe. Her Hollywood career stands as an affirmation of her remarkable capacity and the broad affirmation of her commitment to the world of cinema.

Chapter 4: The Versatile Actress

Dench's capacity to consistently move between sorts, characters, and mediums has cemented her status as a genuine artist chameleon.

Range of Characters and Acting Styles

All through her decades-long travel within the world of theater and film, she has consistently transitioned between an endless run of characters and investigated various acting procedures, taking off a permanent stamp on the performing arts.

One of Dench's most striking properties as a performing artist is her chameleon-like capacity to possess assorted characters over diverse classes and periods. She has depicted everything from Shakespearean champions like Woman Macbeth and Ruler

Gertrude to modern figures in movies such as "Iris" and "Notes on an Embarrassment." Her uncommon extent has permitted her to handle both comedic and emotional parts with rise to artfulness. Dench's depiction of Ruler Victoria in "Mrs. Brown" showcased her superb deportment, whereas her portrayal of M within the James Bond establishment demonstrated her capacity to play solid, definitive characters.

Acting isn't just almost conveying lines; it's about encapsulating the substance of a character, and Dench has reliably exceeded expectations in this angle. Her devotion to understanding the motivations, foundations, and passionate complexities of her characters is clear within the profundity of her exhibitions. She includes a surprising talent for passing on a character's inward turmoil or bliss through unobtrusive facial expressions and body dialect, making a true association between the group of onlookers and the characters she brings to life.

Furthermore, Dench's acting fashion has advanced with the changing scene of theater and cinema. She consistently adjusted to the requests of both organize and screen, displaying her flexibility. On arrange, her commanding nearness and effective voice have made her a drive to be figured within Shakespearean preparations. Her film work has highlighted her capacity to communicate perplexing feelings and subtleties through close-up shots, making her exhibitions similarly captivating in more insinuating settings.

Dench's commitment to her craft is clear within the broad inquiry she embraces for each part. Whether it's submerging herself in verifiable records for a period show or examining real-life figures for a historical part, she saves no effort in her journey for genuineness. This commitment to her characters has earned her various grants and honors, counting a few prestigious Olivier Grants and an Academy Award for her part in "Shakespeare in Love."

In essence, Judi Dench's career could be a confirmation of her unparalleled extent of characters and her capacity to adjust to different acting styles. Her work has not as it were improved the world of excitement but has moreover set a standard of brilliance for yearning on-screen characters, emphasizing the significance of flexibility, commitment, and a profound understanding of the human condition within the craftsmanship of acting.

Her bequest as a performing artist will without a doubt proceed to rouse eras of entertainers to come.

Awards and Critical Acclaim

Judi Dench's career has been checked by plenty of grants, awards, and basic approval, building her up as one of the foremost celebrated and respected performing artists in the history of both arrange and screen. Her earth-shattering capacity and dedication to her make have dependably accumulated praise from faultfinders, peers, and bunches of spectators alike.

On the sensational organize, Dench's travel began with her a long time inside the Distinguished Shakespeare Company (RSC). Her uncommon presentations in Shakespearean classics like "Romeo and

Juliet," "Town," and "Macbeth" earned her a distant coming to acknowledge. Faultfinders praised her capacity to bring depth, nuance, and realness to her characters, making her a standout nearness within the world of theater.

Transitioning to film, Dench kept on fascinating gatherings of people and pundits with her compelling exhibitions.

One of her breakthrough minutes on the huge screen came with her part as Ruler Victoria in "Mrs. Brown" (1997), which earned her a Foundation Grant designation for Best On-screen character. This assignment stamped the starting of an exceptional streak of Institute Grant acknowledgment for her.

Her depiction of Ruler Elizabeth I in "Shakespeare in Cherish" (1998) secured her first Foundation Grant win, taking home the Oscar for Best Supporting On-screen character. This was a turning point in her career because it catapulted her to universal fame. Dench's capacity to communicate complex feelings with nuance and beauty set her apart in an industry known for its competitive nature.

In addition to her Oscar win, Dench got various assignments and grants for her film work, including Brilliant Globe Grants, BAFTA Grants, and Screen Performing Artists Society Grants. Her collaborations with executives like Stephen Frears and Richard Eyre led to a few of her most paramount exhibitions in movies such as "Philomena" (2013), "Notes on an Outrage" (2006), and "Iris" (2001).

Beyond the silver screen, Dench's arranged nearness remained a drive to be figured with. Her depiction of Queen Elizabeth II in "The Gathering of People" (2013) on Broadway and in London's West Conclusion was met with broad approval and garnered her a Tony Grant for Best On-screen Character in a Play. This accomplishment set her status as an artist of unparalleled talent.

Throughout her career, Judi Dench's capacity to consistently move between theater and film has been a confirmation of her flexibility as a performing artist. Her exhibitions in both mediums have not only earned her basic recognition but have enhanced the creative scene of both industries.

In acknowledgment of her commitments to the expressions, Dench has received various lifetime accomplishment grants and respects, advancing and underscoring her status as a beloved and regarded figure within the world of entertainment. Her persevering request, coupled with her unwavering commitment to her creation, cements Judi Dench's bequest as a genuine symbol within the domain of acting, winning her a put among the all-time greats.

Chapter 5: Personal Life

Within the world of excitement, where the highlight regularly obscures the line between open and private, Judi Dench has overseen reserving a smooth adjustment between her individual life and her thriving career. This chapter dives into the complexities of her world, giving knowledge into the lady behind the famous parts.

Relationships and Family

Judi Dench's existence within the highlight is not as distinguished by her famous performing job but also by her profound affiliations with her family and cherished ones. Whereas she may be famous for her outstanding skills on stage and screen, her existence has been similarly notable.

Throughout her life, she has kept up a close-knit and solid family. Her family gave the establishment for her early years, fostering her love for expressiveness and books.

Judi's links with her clan have moreover played a crucial element in her life. She had a more seasoned brother, Jeffery Dench, who was a performing artist and author himself. Jeffery's impact and direction certainly led to Judi's early interest in acting and her choice to seek it as a vocation. Their mutual interest in the theater established a one-of-a-kind friendship between them.

In 1971, Judi Dench married performing artist Michael Williams, and their union became one of the foremost persevering and respected in British theater and movies. Their marriage continued for 30 years until

Michael's unexpected departure in 2001. During their time together, they consistently collaborated on organizing and filming, growing to be an adored acting couple. Their relationship was checked by common regard and admiration, and their on-screen chemistry was highly lauded.

Judi and Michael moreover discussed the delights and hardships of parenting a family. They had one girl, Tara Cressida Frances Williams, born in 1972. Despite the demands of their vocations, they were committed guardians and attempted to preserve a solid and cherishing home existence for their girl. Tara went on to take after her parents' strides, searching for a profession in performing.

The misfortune of Michael was a vital minute in Judi's life, and it without a doubt had a persistent influence on her. Be that as it may, she proceeded to locate comfort and reinforcement in her family and near pals. Her fortitude and assurance to keep working and contribute to the world of excitement are a confirmation of her inside quality and the back structure she has established over the years.

In overview, Judi Dench's relationships and family have been required for her voyage through life within the spotlight. From her near friendship with her brother and the enduring love she shared with Michael Williams to her role as a mother, her associations have formed her as much as her unexpected career. These profound ties have offered her a sturdy foundation, permitting her to dazzle not only as an on-screen figure but also as an individual of wonderful character and judgment.

Balancing Fame with Privacy

Celebrities like Judi Dench, who have received accolades and recognition on a global scale, find it extremely difficult to balance fame with seclusion. Even if the frequent prying and interference in their private lives might be debilitating, protecting their right to privacy is still crucial for their well-being. Here is a thorough examination of how Judi Dench has managed this delicate balance throughout her illustrious career.

Judi Dench's work in the entertainment sector helped her reach the pinnacles of fame. She has won countless honors for her incredible talent, including an Academy

Award, six BAFTAs, and many Laurence Olivier Awards. Her life has consequently attracted a lot of media and public curiosity. For superstars who frequently find themselves under the spotlight round-the-clock, this condition is prevalent.

Dench has always been guarded of her private life, despite the attraction of fame. She is aware of the value of preserving solitude and normalcy in the middle of stardom's upheaval. Rather than being motivated by secrecy, this need for seclusion is a result of the need for a haven from the ongoing attention that comes with being a public figure.

Dench has achieved this equilibrium in part by keeping her private affairs mainly hidden from the public view. She avoids the harsh media spotlight by hardly ever bringing up her family or personal relationships in interviews. She would rather draw attention away from her personal life by letting her work and craft do the talking.

Furthermore, Dench uses social media and public appearances with restraint and purpose. When necessary, she interacts with the public and her supporters to promote her work or raise money for charitable causes. She can keep some control over her public image thanks to this planned interaction while also engaging her audience.

Furthermore, Judi Dench's excellent sense of professionalism has helped her strike a balance between popularity and solitude. She has an unshakeable commitment to her career and makes sure that her performances come first, not her personal life. She has developed a reputation as a master artist by constantly producing excellent work and putting her craft first.

Judi Dench's strategy is a helpful illustration in a society where celebrities' right to privacy is getting harder to come by. Her perseverance and fortitude are demonstrated by her capacity to be true to herself, put her well-being first, and safeguard her private life. Dench proves that maintaining a healthy work-life balance is achievable even in the glamorous world of show business and that popularity should not come at the expense of one's privacy.

Chapter 6: Later Career

Judi Dench continued to enthrall audiences on the stage and in films as she entered the later part of her brilliant career. Her commitment to her art and amazing adaptability made sure her impact on the entertainment industry never diminished.

Continuing Success on Stage and Screen

Judi Dench's continuing success in theater and movies is corroborated by her outstanding bestowal and unappeasable devotion to the acting trade. She has easily changed between these two stripes throughout her staid career, having a profound jolt on each. On the theater stage, Dench's career has been less than fabulous. She spent her early moments as a member of the Royal Shakespeare Company(RSC), which helped her hone her capacities and produce a commanding dramatic presence. Her representations of well-known Shakespearean characters, to analogous Lady Macbeth in" Macbeth" and Ophelia in " Hamlet," revealed her command of Bard's notations. She received a lot of accolades and cemented her character as one of the swish stage impersonators of her generation because of her capability to gracefully achieve Shakespearean verse and bring daedal characters to life. Indeed after having a prosperous career in movies, Dench Norway stopped enjoying the theater. She appeared in the current factory and plays in extension to Shakespeare's classics, establishing her strictness as an actress. She won solace for her definition of Queen Victoria in"Mrs. Brown " on stage and also in the movie adaptation, proving her art at zipping between mediums. In the world of filmland, Judi Dench has made a name for herself. She has played several characters in films of nonidentical stripes, which serves as a substantiation of her versatility in her filmography. By bringing starkness and intelligence to the portion of M in the James Bond movie series, she earned the petals of the cult. She was honored with the Academy Award for Stylish Supporting Actress for her definition of Queen Elizabeth I in " Shakespeare in Love," proving her prowess in nonfictional plays. One of Dench's defining characteristics as a player is how reahreshowllydaptably she can convey a wide range of passions. She's able to deeply connect with the cult during her performances thanks to her keen understanding of mortal nature. n matter the portion she's rollicking — a regal queen, a grieving widow, or a sardonic teacher — Dench delivers rich performances with a passionate jolt. Some of her most well-known work has also reacted from her cooperation with administrators like Stephen Frears, who directed her in" Philomena," and Richard Eyre, who directed her in" Notes on a Reproach." She has made a name for herself as a portion model for aspiring impersonators by taking challenging places and constantly going against the grain of morals and prospects. Judi Dench's acting career is substantiated by her unvarying devotion to the craft, letch to take on delicate places, and unusual capability to conserve spectators' concentration whether she acts on stage or in front of the camera. Her contributions to theater and filmland left a continuing influence, and her ongoing success serves as a relief to impersonators and actresses all around the world.

Iconic Roles in the 21st Century

In the 21st century, Dame Judi Dench continued to appeal to the cult with a series of iconic places that showcased her unrivaled gift and versatility as an actress. Her capability to seamlessly transition between stripes and characters further solidified her status as a cinematic legend. One of her name performances came in the form of " Iris"(2001), a biographical drama in which Dench portrayed the acclaimed British novelist and champion Iris Murdoch. Her definition of Murdoch, who was tortured by Alzheimer's complaint, was deeply moving and emotionally sonorous. Dench's capability to convey the profound struggles of a brilliant mind in decline earned her critical sun and her fifth Academy Award nomination. Dench also graced the tableware screen as M in the James Bond ballot, beginning with" GoldenEye"(1995) and continuing throughout the 21st century. Her definition of the stern yet maternal head of MI6 added depth and gravitas to the series. Her presence in films like" Skyfall"(2012) and" Spectre"(2015) showcased her enduring appeal to both new and longtime Bond suckers. In "Mrs. Henderson Presents"(2005), Dench again demonstrated her capability to seamlessly blend humor and heart. She played the nominal character,

Laura Henderson, an eccentric widow who, during World War II, transforms a London theater into a venue for raw revues. Dench's performance brought charm and wit to the character, earning her yet another Academy Award nomination. Also, her part as Queen Victoria in " Victoria & Abdul"(2017) offered a fresh perspective on the ultimate times of the monarch's life. The film explored the doubtful fellowship between Queen Victoria and her Indian companion, Abdul Karim. Dench's definition of Victoria stressed her capability to convey regal grace while probing into the complications of a character's emotional trip. Judi Dench's impact on the 21st-century cinematic terrain extended beyond traditional places. She advanced her voice to various animated films, including the cherished" The

Chronicles of Riddick" series, where she raised the character Aereon, adding her distinguished oral bent to the realm of wisdom fabrication. Throughout the 21st century, her iconic places demonstrated her deep devotion to her craft and her capability to breathe life into a nonidentical batch of characters.

Her progressive presence on screen continued to inspire all. Not only that. It solidifies her heritage as one of the most reputed and cherished actresses in the world.

Chapter 7: Philanthropy and Advocacy

Throughout her outstanding career, Judi Dench not only graced the stage and movie with her unusual gift but also devoted a significant portion of her life to philanthropy and advocacy.

Causes and Charitable Work

Throughout her outstanding career, Judi Dench has been not only a celebrated actress but also a devoted supporter of numerous charitable antecedents. Her passion for philanthropy and humanitarian work reflects her deep sense of compassion and her desire to exercise her platform for positive change. One of Judi Dench's noble philanthropic trials has been her involvement with various charitable corporations dedicated to medical disquisition and healthcare. She has advanced her brace to a cancer acquisition company, analogous to Cancer Research UK, and has exercised her influence to elate awareness and finances for the treatment and prevention of this disastrous complaint. Dench's contributions have helped advance medical wisdom and improve the lives of innumerable identities affected by cancer. In addition to her work in the healthcare region, Dench has been a passionate supporter of wildlife conservation. She has been associated with corporations like the World Wildlife Fund(WWF) and the Born Free Foundation, laboriously participating in campaigns leveled at protecting exposed species and husbanding their homes. Her passion for environmental antecedents highlights her company for the well-being of the planet and its inhabitants beyond the mortal race. Also, Judi Dench has supported the cause of children's welfare and instruction. She has supported charities that give instruction and openings for dented children, both in the United Kingdom and internationally. Her efforts have helped depressed youth break up the circle of poverty and achieve a brilliant future through access to quality instruction and essential resources. Dench's charitable work extends to the trades as well. She has been a hot supporter of cultural institutions, such as the Royal Academy of Dramatic Art(RADA) and the Shakespeare Schools Foundation, which were cast to nurture immature bestowal in the performing trades.

Her contributions to these corporations have consoled that aspiring impersonators and artists have access to the training and resources necessary to trace their conceits. In moments of crisis and debacle, Judi Dench has not wavered to advance her brace. Whether it's through fundraising efforts or participating in relief missions, she has constantly demonstrated her passion for helping communities in need. Her humanitarian work during events like natural disasters and global heads showcases her compassion and dedication to making a positive jolt in the lives of those facing adversity.

In conclusion, Judi Dench's charitable work spans a wide spectrum of antecedents, reflecting her nonidentical interests and unvarying passion for making the world a better situation. Her contributions to medical disquisition, wildlife conservation, children's welfare, the trades, and debacle relief have left an indelible mark on numerous charitable corporations and the lives of innumerable identities. Dench's philanthropic efforts are substantiated by her belief in exercising fame and influence as a force for good, embodying the paragon that a life in the spotlight can also be a life of purpose and positive change.

Social and Political Engagement

Judi Dench's social and political engagement throughout her life has been a testament to her fidelity to using her platform and influence for positive change. While she's primarily known for her remarkable amusement career, her commitment to colorful causes has left an unforgettable mark beyond the tableware screen. One of the causes closest to her heart is the fight against HIV/ AIDS. Dench has been laboriously involved in raising mindfulness and finances for associations devoted to combating the HIV/ AIDS epidemic. She became a patron of the Terrence Higgins Trust, a leading HIV charity in the UK, and worked lifelessly to reduce the smirch associated with the complaint. Her advocacy played a pivotal part in destigmatizing HIV/ AIDS and ensuring that those affected admit the support and care they need. In addition to her work in healthcare, Dench has been an oral advocate for environmental conservation. She supported enterprises aimed at guarding wildlife and conserving natural territories. Her involvement in environmental causes demonstrates her commitment to addressing global issues and promoting sustainability. On the political front, Dench has Norway nestled down from expressing her views on important social and political matters. She has used her platform to advocate for equivalency and mortal rights. Dench has been an oral supporter of LGBTQ rights and marriage equivalency. Her advocacy in this area has contributed to positive changes in societal stations and legislation. Likewise, she has advanced her voice to juggernauts against ethical demarcation and internationalism. Dench's commitment to inclusivity and diversity is apparent not only in her acting choices but also in her active involvement in movements seeking a further indifferent and just society. Judi Dench's social and political engagement goes beyond bare countersign; she has used her celebrity status to amplify important issues and inspire change. Her fidelity to these causes demonstrates that she isn't just a talented actress but also a compassionate and socially conscious individual who has made a meaningful impact on society through her advocacy. Dench's heritage extends beyond her cinematic achievements, leaving a lasting print as an inexhaustible advocate for positive social change.

Chapter 8: Legacy

Having spent over six decades on both stage and screen, Dench has left an unforgettable mark on the world of theater and film.

Influence on Theater and Film

Judi Dench's influence on both theater and film is nothing short of extraordinary, leaving an unforgettable mark on both art forms throughout her outstanding career. Her impact can be felt in colorful aspects, from her outstanding performances to her advocacy for the trades. In the realm of theater, Dench's benefactions are bottomless. She's extensively regarded as one of the topmost stage actresses of her generation. Her early times with the Royal Shakespeare Company(RSC) allowed her to hone her craft and establish herself as a redoubtable gift in classical theater. Her depiction of iconic Shakespearean characters, similar to Lady Macbeth and Cleopatra, showcased her unequaled capability to breathe life into complex laces. Dench's commitment to the theater extended beyond her emotional performances. She became an advocate for the preservation of the trades and the significance of live theater. Her involvement with the RSC and other theater companies helped ensure the durability of classical theater traditions, and she inspired numerous aspiring actors to pursue careers on the stage. In the realm of film, Judi Dench's influence is inversely profound. Her transition from the stage to the screen was flawless, and she snappily established herself as a protean actress able to dive into a wide range of places. Her depiction of

Queen Victoria in"Mrs. Brown"(1997) earned her critical sun and her first Academy Award nomination, motioning her capability to exceed in both literal and contemporary places. Dench's most iconic contribution to film came with her depiction of M, the head of MI6, in the James Bond film series. Her character added depth and gravitas to the ballot, and her on-screen presence became synonymous with authority and complication. Her performances in Bond flicks, similar to" GoldenEye," " Skyfall," and" Casino Royale," garnered wide recognition and contributed to the enduring fashionability of the series. Beyond her acting prowess, Dench's influence in film extended to her advocacy for gender equivalency and recognition of aged actors. She was an open advocate for equal pay and openings for women in the film industry, slipping light on the gender difference that persisted in Hollywood. Also, her uninterrupted success in film well into her times challenged ageist stations in the assiduity and inspired aged actors to pursue meaningful places.

Judi Dench's Enduring Impact

Throughout her outstanding career gauging several decades, she has left an unforgettable mark on both stage and screen. Then, we claw into the colorful angles of her continuing influence.

The Art of Acting

Judi Dench's donation to the craft of acting is bottomless. Her unequaled gift and fidelity have set a standard for excellence that aspiring actors strive to achieve.

Dench's capability to seamlessly transition between theater and film, painlessly portraying characters from colorful backgrounds and ages, has solidified her status as one of the most protean actors in the assiduity. Her profound understanding of character development, nuanced performances, and unvarying commitment to her places continue to inspire actors worldwide.

Shakespearean heritage

Dench's association with the Royal Shakespeare Company and her multitudinous iconic Shakespearean places have made her synonymous with the Bard's work. Her depiction of characters like Lady Macbeth, Cleopatra, and Titania has come out fabulous. She has not only brought these characters to life but has also introduced

Shakespeare's dateless stories to new generations, icing their applicability for times to come.

Breaking walls

Throughout her career, Judi Dench has broken down gender and age walls in the entertainment industry. She has shown that gift and skill aren't bound by age or gender, proving that actresses can have thriving careers well into their aftertimes. Dench has become a symbol of commission for women in the assiduity, emphasizing the significance of gift, adaptability, and passion over societal prospects.

Mentorship and Inspiration Dench's influence extends beyond her performances. She has served as a tutor and source of alleviation for numerous actors, directors, and artists. Her wisdom and liberality in participating with her goals and knowledge have shaped the careers of numerous aspiring bents. Her commitment to nurturing the coming generation of artists ensures that her heritage will continue through the work of those she has inspired.

Charitable and Advocacy Work

Beyond her cultural benefactions, Judi Dench's enduring impact can be seen in her humanitarian sweat and advocacy work. She has been an oral advocate for causes similar to the fight against macular degeneration, using her fame to raise mindfulness and finances for exploration. Her fidelity to social and political issues highlights the eventuality for artists to make a meaningful impact beyond the stage and screen.

In conclusion, Judi Dench's enduring impact is a testament to her extraordinary gift, fidelity, and the profound influence she has had on the world of theater and film. Her heritage serves as a lamp for unborn generations of artists, reminding them of the transformative power of liars and the enduring significance of the performing trades. Dench's benefactions will continue to shape the entertainment industry and inspire cults and artists likewise for generations to come.

Conclusion

In" Judi Dench A Life in the Spotlight," we have traced the remarkable trip of an artist who, for over six decades, has illuminated the stage and movie with her unrivaled bestowal, indulgence, and unwavering dedication. Dame Judi Dench's life in the spotlight is not precisely a commentary of an outstanding career; it's a corroboration of the authority of passion, rigidity, and artistic veracity. From her early days walking the boards of the Royal Shakespeare Company to her transformative presence in Hollywood, Judi Dench has embodied the substance of a true thespian. Her capability to inhabit a myriad of characters with actuality and depth, excelling in time and order, has earned her a position among the pantheon of acting keys. Beyond her art,

Judi Dench's life is a corroboration of her unvarying devotion to her craft and her profound influence on the world of theater and cinema. Her rubric is not precisely the sum of her numerous accolades and awards but the indelible mark she has left on the very soul of the performing trades. Her advocacy for the conservation of theater, her dedication to charitable antecedents, and her outspokenness on effects near to her heart are all angles of a life lived with purpose and satisfaction. Yet, as we close the chapter on this exploration of Judi Dench's life, we are reminded that indeed the brightest stars in the firmament must eventually cloak. Dame Judi Dench, in all her brilliance, is no expostulation to the inexorable march of time. Still, her rubric will ever shine, like a celestial beacon, inspiring conceptions of impersonators and artists to reach for the stars and follow in her way. In the spotlight, Dame Judi Dench has radiated brighter than utmost, not exclusively as an actress, but as a hallmark of tenacity, actuality, and the everlasting pursuit of distinction. Her story is corroboration to the transformative authority of the trades and the continuing jolt of a life lived with passion and purpose. As the cope falls on this bio, we are left with the resonance of Dame Judi Dench's life, a story that continues to appeal to and inspire, reminding us that the spotlight can illuminate not only a stage but the true substance of our souls.

Reflection on a Remarkable Career

Judi Dench's distinguished lifetime traverses north of sixty years, making a permanent imprint on the universe of theater, film, and TV. As we think about her wonderful journey, a few key perspectives stick out, characterizing her inheritance as one of the best entertainers of her age.

Flexibility

Judi Dench's adaptability as an entertainer is completely bewildering. She easily changed between exemplary Shakespearean jobs on the stage to current, complex characters on screen. Her capacity to submerge herself in different jobs exhibited her unrivaled reach and profundity as a craftsman.

The Force of the Stage

Dench's initial years were dominatingly centered around the stage, where she sharpened her specialty. Her Shakespearean exhibitions, specifically, were praised for their credibility and profound profundity. Her depiction of Woman Macbeth, for example, passed on crowds in wonder at her capacity to convey the person's intricacy and internal conflict.

Filmic Wins

While she had proactively laid down a good foundation for herself as a theater symbol, Judi Dench's introduction to film brought her overall acknowledgment. Her exhibitions in films like "Shakespeare in Affection" and "Mrs. Brown" procured her basic recognition and various honors, including a Foundation Grant for Best Supporting Entertainer. Dench's presence in the cinema was a demonstration of her perseverance through allure and versatility.

Tastefulness and Beauty

All through her vocation, Woman Judi Dench held herself with a feeling of class and elegance that reached out past her exhibitions. Her great disposition and ready presence on and off the stage and screen acquired her the love and profound respect of fans and associates alike.

Conquering Difficulties

Dench's profession was not without its difficulties. Well-being mishaps, for example, her fight with macular degeneration, took steps to diminish her acting profession. Nonetheless, her assurance to keep performing, even with restricted visual perception, exhibited her strength and steady enthusiasm for her specialty.

Generosity and Backing

Past her acting gifts, Judi Dench's devotion to generous makes and activism featured her responsibility to make the world a superior spot. Her association with different beneficent undertakings and backing for compassion layer her into existence.

Effect on People in the Future

Woman Judi Dench's effect on hopeful entertainers and entertainers couldn't possibly be more significant. Her work keeps on rousing new ages of entertainers, empowering them to take a stab at greatness and flexibility in their vocations.

All in all, Judi Dench's exceptional profession is a demonstration of her creativity, flexibility, and ability to get through her obligation to the universe of diversion. Her capacity to spellbind crowds on both stage and screen, combined with her beauty and generous endeavors, cement her as a genuine symbol. As we think about her life at the center of attention, it's clear that Lady Judi Dench's inheritance will keep on sparkling brilliantly for a long time into the future.

Contributions to the Arts

Judi Dench's commitments to human expression are downright outstanding. Through her distinguished lifetime, she lastingly affected both the theater and entertainment worlds, procuring her a spot among the most loved and compelling figures in human expression. Here are a portion of her key commitments:

Theater Greatness

Judi Dench's initial profession was essentially established in the theater. Her wonderful ability and commitment to the art have procured her standing as one of the best stage entertainers of her age.

She has taken on a large number of notable jobs in works of art and contemporary plays, exhibiting her flexibility as an entertainer.

Her depiction of Shakespearean characters, including Woman Macbeth and Cleopatra, has been especially celebrated and has set a norm for greatness in traditional theater.

Film Change

Dench's progress from the stage to film denoted a huge change in her vocation. She carried similar force and expertise to her film jobs, raising the nature of exhibitions in the business.

Her work in films like "Shakespeare in Adoration" (for which she won a Foundation Grant), "Philomena," and the James Bond series as M, acquainted her with a more extensive worldwide crowd, establishing her status as a true-to-life legend.

Spearheading Ladies in Film

Judi Dench has been a pioneer for ladies in film. Her capacity to get driving jobs in significant movies, even in her later years, tested age and orientation generalizations in the business.

She has been a motivation for yearning for entertainers, demonstrating that ability and expertise are imperishable and that ladies can be strong figures in both acting and filmmaking.

Advancement of Shakespeare

Dench's profound association with crafted William Shakespeare has prompted her dynamic advancement of his plays and their significance in the social scene.

She has been associated with different Shakespearean creations and has loaned her voice to narratives and activities pointed toward making Shakespeare open to more extensive crowds.

Backing for Human expression

All through her profession, Dench has been an energetic backer for human expression, perceiving their fundamental job in the public eye. She has upheld various expressions, associations, and drives pointed toward sustaining ability and protecting the imaginative legacy.

Instructive Drives

She has likewise been engaged in instructive endeavors to rouse the up-and-coming age of specialists. Her commitments reach past the stage and screen, as she has effectively taken part in coaching youthful entertainers and entertainers.

Printed in Great Britain
by Amazon